For Lee Hopkins, my wild friend
–J. Y.

For my daddy, who taught me that learning is not only important, but a joy
–H. E. Y. S.

In memory of David Christopher Touchton
–R. R.

ACKNOWLEDGMENTS

The Publisher gratefully thanks Brad Clough, Assistant Professor of Asian Studies and Religion, Bard College, and Padma Kaimal, Assistant Professor of Art and Art History, Colgate University, for their kind assistance.

SIMON & SCHUSTER BOOKS FOR YOUNG READERS
An imprint of Simon & Schuster Children's Publishing Division
1230 Avenue of the Americas, New York, New York 10020
Text copyright © 2001 by Jane Yolen and
Heidi Elisabet Yolen Stemple
Illustrations copyright © 2001 by Roger Roth
All rights reserved including the right of reproduction in whole or in part in any form. SIMON & SCHUSTER BOOKS FOR YOUNG READERS is a trademark of Simon & Schuster. Book design by Paul Zakris. The text of this book is set in 14-point Minister Book.
Printed in Hong Kong
10 9 8 7 6 5 4 3 2 1

LIBRARY OF CONGRESS CARD NUMBER: 00-111050
ISBN 0-689-81080-6

first edition

A NOTE FROM THE ARTIST

The illustrations in this book were done in a series of stages. First I did tiny, rough "thumbnail" sketches. This is really the fun and creative part for me. Then, from these thumbnails I made large, detailed pencil drawings, which I traced onto watercolor paper. Next, I painted the picture using transparent watercolor, adding pencil for detail and texture.

BIBLIOGRAPHY

Aitchison, Jean. *The Articulate Mammal.* New York: Universe Books, 1977.

Eisler, Robert. *Man into Wolf.* Santa Barbara: Ross-Erikson, Inc., Publishers, 1978.

Fiennes, Richard. *The Order of Wolves.* Indianapolis: Bobbs-Merrill, 1976.

Lane, Harlan, and Richard Pillard. *The Wild Boy of Burundi.* New York: Random House, 1978.

Maclean, Charles. *The Wolf Children.* New York: Hill and Wang, 1977.

Mech, L. David. *The Wolf.* Garden City, NY: The American Museum of Natural History/The Natural History Press, 1970.

Singh, the Reverend J. A. L., and Professor Robert M. Zingg. *Wolf-Children and Feral Man.* New York: Harper & Brothers Publishers, 1939.

THE Wolf Girls

AN UNSOLVED MYSTERY FROM HISTORY

By Jane Yolen and

Heidi Elisabet Yolen Stemple

Illustrated by Roger Roth

Simon & Schuster Books for Young Readers
New York London Toronto Sydney Singapore

When I grow up I want to be a detective, just like my dad. He says I was curious from the day I was born, which is all right with me since curious is just what a detective needs to be.

In my father's office is a file of old mysteries that have never been solved. Boy, am I curious about them! The police call these cases "open," but Dad and I call them "mysteries from history." I am determined to figure them out.

For each of these unsolved mysteries, I research as much as I can. In a notebook, I highlight the most important clues. Sometimes I draw maps. Sometimes I use time lines. And sometimes I have to look up words that are special to the case.

The Wolf Girls is about two girls in an orphanage in India in the 1920s. It was believed by many people at the time that the girls had been raised by wolves, because they ran on all fours and ate raw meat. But some people believed otherwise. No one is sure. My dad says no mystery is impossible to solve as long as you have enough clues.

This is how the story goes.

INDIA

At the edge of the great Indian sal forest,
where peacocks dance among the trees,
lay the village of Midnapore.
Half a mile from the railway station
and surrounded by a brushwood fence
was "The Home," an orphanage run by
the Reverend J. A. L. Singh.
Early in September 1921,
the local doctor, S. P. Sarbadhicari,
came to examine two very sick girls.
According to Singh, the girls had been left
on his doorstep a year before by a sadhu.

Joseph Singh was a missionary eager to move up within the church. While studying at Calcutta University, he married against the traditional views of his parents. By doing so, he lost a large sum of money he was to inherit.

There were sixteen children living in Singh's orphanage in 1920. Some he had discovered homeless and starving in rural villages. Others—mostly handicapped or unwanted girls from extremely poor tribes—had been found abandoned in fields or forests. Those children would likely have starved or been eaten by tigers or wolves.

SAL FOREST: a jungle of sal (or shal) trees so thick that the leaves make a green canopy

BRUSHWOOD: a fence made of laced branches

ORPHANAGE: a group home where children without parents or other relatives are cared for

SADHU: a Hindu holy man

VILLAGERS: A group of people who settle in a particular area.

TRIBE: A group of people who often wander from one bit of wasteland to another.

Dr. Sarbadhicari treated the girls with common drugs, especially sulfur powder, which forced out great quantities of intestinal worms. But the younger girl also had a disease called nephritis. The sulfur damaged her kidneys, which had already been weakened by the disease. Antibiotics had not been invented yet.

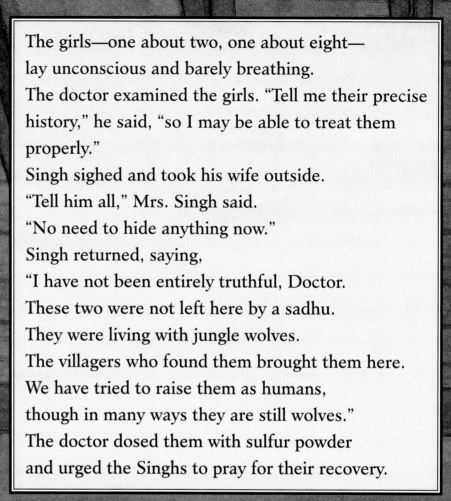

The girls—one about two, one about eight—
lay unconscious and barely breathing.
The doctor examined the girls. "Tell me their precise
history," he said, "so I may be able to treat them
properly."
Singh sighed and took his wife outside.
"Tell him all," Mrs. Singh said.
"No need to hide anything now."
Singh returned, saying,
"I have not been entirely truthful, Doctor.
These two were not left here by a sadhu.
They were living with jungle wolves.
The villagers who found them brought them here.
We have tried to raise them as humans,
though in many ways they are still wolves."
The doctor dosed them with sulfur powder
and urged the Singhs to pray for their recovery.

From Singh's annual missionary report, 1921:

"It is pleasing to note, in writing this report, one uncommon instance regarding two inmates of this institution. We might mention it here and trust it will create an interest among our friends, that we have rescued two wolf-girls . . . secured from wolf dens by villagers in the jungle. . . . In bringing the report of the year to a conclusion, we call attention to the urgent financial need in support of such an institution."

GOSSIP: a person who talks about other people's affairs

GAWK: to stare at stupidly

Although the Singhs begged him
to keep the children's background secret,
Dr. Sarbadhicari was a terrible gossip.
He told everyone about the wolf girls.
When the younger girl died on September 21,
a newspaper carried an article about them,
based on Dr. Sarbadhicari's comments.
Even the servants at The Home talked to reporters.
Singh was furious with them all,
but his wife reminded him that he himself had
written about the girls in his missionary report.
On October 1, Singh invited the townspeople
to view the remaining wolf girl.
They gawked as if she were an extraordinary beast.
Regular visiting hours were established,
and though no admission was charged,
Singh did not discourage donations
that helped finance the running of The Home.

Singh did not keep a journal at first. He started taking notes a year after the girls were rescued, and someone else typed them. Although Singh was a university-educated man, one expert said the journal was full of "contradictions, muddled thinking, broken English, and poor spelling. . . ." Singh wanted to publish the journal with its twenty-two fuzzy black-and-white snapshots of the girls to make money for The Home, but it took him eighteen years to do it. Largely eaten by termites, the original journal is now unreadable, but it is still the only eyewitness account of the girls.

Singh was now a celebrity of sorts.
He felt it was time to tell the story fully.
Not the first story:
that the children, left by a sadhu,
had been abandoned on his steps.
Not the second story:
that villagers rescued the girls from wolves.
But a third story in which he was the hero.
He created a journal,
dating it as if he were writing it
at the moment the girls were rescued,
and not a year later.
The diary begins with Singh traveling
by bullock cart from The Home
through the sal forest
to the little village of Godamuri,
trying to convert the local tribes to Christianity.

Singh's journal said that in Godamuri,
the villagers spoke of a nearby man-ghost.
Since Singh was known as a holy man,
they asked him to drive off the ghost.
Singh agreed, knowing that good Christian prayer
would be his weapon against a ghost.
But just in case, he kept his rifle close at hand.
Singh and his men were led
deep into the forest to a small clearing
near a two-story-high termite mound.
There was no sign of the creature.
Later in his journal, Singh wrote:
"Sept. 24: I thought it was all false
and did not care much."
He did not expect to hear about the ghost again.
He was wrong.

Termite, or white ant, mounds are found in many parts of India and other tropical countries. The average mound rises five or six feet high over a central cavern, though the one near Godamuri was more than twelve feet tall. Jungle animals often make dens in abandoned mounds.

In the 1920s most of the people living in small villages in India believed in many kinds of ghosts or spirits. They would offer up special prayers and offerings so the ghost or spirit would leave them alone.

MOHUA: a type of fig tree found in India

LANGUR: a slender, long-tailed Asian monkey

CICADA: a grasshopper-like insect with a shrill, chirping call

From Singh's journal: "Close after the cubs came the ghost—a hideous-looking being—hand, foot, and body like a human being; but the head was a big ball of something covering the shoulders and the upper portion of the bust. . . ."

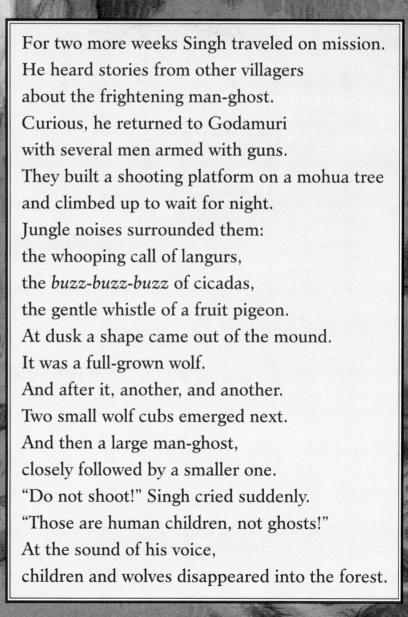

For two more weeks Singh traveled on mission.
He heard stories from other villagers
about the frightening man-ghost.
Curious, he returned to Godamuri
with several men armed with guns.
They built a shooting platform on a mohua tree
and climbed up to wait for night.
Jungle noises surrounded them:
the whooping call of langurs,
the *buzz-buzz-buzz* of cicadas,
the gentle whistle of a fruit pigeon.
At dusk a shape came out of the mound.
It was a full-grown wolf.
And after it, another, and another.
Two small wolf cubs emerged next.
And then a large man-ghost,
closely followed by a smaller one.
"Do not shoot!" Singh cried suddenly.
"Those are human children, not ghosts!"
At the sound of his voice,
children and wolves disappeared into the forest.

The Indian wolf looks similar to a jackal. It is smaller, slighter, and has a thinner coat than the American wolf. Cubs live on milk for about two weeks, then eat food that their mother partially digests and regurgitates. When food is scarce, wolves have been known to prey on domestic animals. According to local records of the time, Indian wolves killed more humans than any other jungle animal. Even recent newspapers carry accounts of Indian wolves carrying off small children.

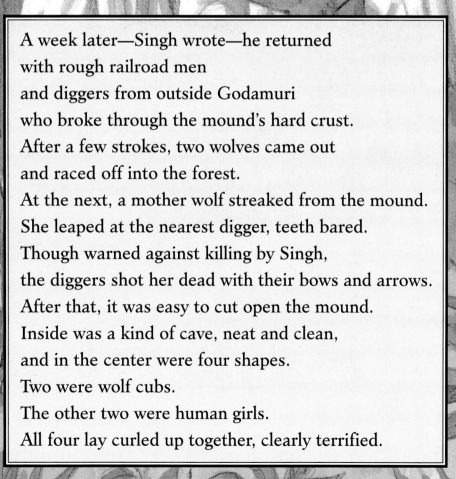

A week later—Singh wrote—he returned
with rough railroad men
and diggers from outside Godamuri
who broke through the mound's hard crust.
After a few strokes, two wolves came out
and raced off into the forest.
At the next, a mother wolf streaked from the mound.
She leaped at the nearest digger, teeth bared.
Though warned against killing by Singh,
the diggers shot her dead with their bows and arrows.
After that, it was easy to cut open the mound.
Inside was a kind of cave, neat and clean,
and in the center were four shapes.
Two were wolf cubs.
The other two were human girls.
All four lay curled up together, clearly terrified.

From Singh's journal: "I sprinkled cold water on their faces. . . . I tried to make them drink some hot tea . . . [tearing] up my handkerchief and roll[ing] it up [in]to a wick. I dipped it in the teacup; and when it was well soaked, I put one end into their mouths and the other end remained in the cup. . . . [They sucked] the wick like a baby."

BAMBOO: tree-sized tropical grass with hollow stems

EARTHEN POT: a dish or pot made of baked clay

The wolf cubs were given to the men.
The children were brought to Godamuri
and placed in separate bamboo cages.
They were to be fed rice and water
in two small earthen pots.
A Godamuri man was put in charge of them
until Singh could return
from his missionary travels.
But five days later, when Singh came back,
he found Godamuri deserted.
The villagers, afraid the creatures
were really ghosts, not human,
had run off into the forest.
Still in their cages, the little girls
were starving and near death.

After nursing the two girls back to health,
the Reverend Singh loaded them into the cart
and drove them for eight days
to his orphanage in Midnapore.
But the wolf girls were so weak and emaciated,
they could not move about, so at first
no one outside of the orphanage saw them.
Singh wrote in his journal:
"They were accepted simply as neglected children."

Singh wrote in his journal that the girls were mud-covered, with scratches, scars, and fleas. The heels of their hands were callused from running on all fours. Their ears trembled like a dog's when they were excited. Their brows were bushy and long. Each had arms almost reaching their knees. Their teeth were close-set, uneven, with fine, sharp edges, the canines longer and more pointed than is usual in humans. However, Singh took no scientific measurements and invited no scientists to examine the girls. He took photographs that were fuzzy and indistinct.

Years later, his own daughter, when interviewed, did not remember the distinctive teeth or exceptional ears or terrifically bushy brows.

EMACIATED: thin and feeble due to disease or poor food

NEGLECTED: not taken proper care of

Mrs. Singh bathed the girls and
cut off their matted hair.
Now they looked more human.
She called the younger girl Amala,
the older one Kamala.
Singh wrote that the girls could not stand erect;
they ran on hands and feet; they preferred dark to day.
They ate only raw meat and gnawed on the bones;
they ate beetles and lapped milk from a bowl.
They tore off any clothing they could.
Their eyes had a peculiar blue glare at night.
They howled like dogs but could not speak.
The other orphans feared them
because they scratched and bit.

A feral child is a wild child raised by animals. In
1758 naturalist Carolus Linnaeus listed three
identifying factors:
tetrapus—child runs on all fours
mutus—child is unable to speak
hirsutus—child is very hairy
Although feral children appear in legends and
myths, scientists doubt their existence. Close
examination of so-called feral children has revealed
that each had some existing handicap, such as
deafness, autism, or retardation. Lack of human care
during abandonment usually created further
damage—an inability to speak or walk or learn. Unlike
wolves, humans need years of early nurturing.
Scientists have concluded that even a healthy child
would not survive for long with only an animal
mother.

One year passed.
According to Singh's journal,
the girls learned to tolerate loincloths—normally male
dress—for cleanliness' sake.
They learned to take biscuits from Mrs. Singh's hands,
going back to their own corner to eat.
They enjoyed a mustard oil massage.
In early September 1921,
little Amala died of a sickness.
Kamala lived eight more years at The Home.
She learned to stand upright—a difficult, painful process.
She learned to speak,
though never more than one hundred words.
Slowly she became less like a wild creature,
wearing dresses, using the toilet,
and even being afraid of barking dogs.
Kamala took ill in September 1929.
She died of typhoid fever on November 14.
She was no more than sixteen years old.

Language must be learned before the age of six or seven, or the ability to learn it at all may be lost. Deafness or abuse can cause permanent loss of oral language.

Autism is a disability generally occurring before the age of three. Autistic children lack verbal skills, have trouble interacting with others, and are overly or undersensitive to stimuli. Autistic children tend to have unusual responses to people and attachments to objects, and they resist changes to their routine.

EXPLOITED: to be used for someone else's advantage

HOAX: a plot to deceive or fool

CONDEMNING: expressing strong disapproval

SAVIOR: someone who rescues people from danger

Singh's journal was published in 1939, long after both girls were dead. Mrs. Singh outlived her husband but never wrote a word about the wolf children.

Two investigations (in 1952 and 1975) included interviews with witnesses who had seen Kamala during the viewing times. Author Charles Maclean spoke to a man who actually claimed to have helped capture the girls fifty years earlier.

The Reverend Singh and his wife
said they never wanted the wolf girls exploited,
yet they displayed Kamala to crowds of visitors.
They said they wanted no one to know about the girls,
but Singh wrote a journal he tried to get published.
By 1926, major newspapers throughout the world
reported regularly about Amala and Kamala.
People argued hotly about whether or not it was a hoax—
two men in a London club even came to blows.
Letters arrived at The Home weekly about the girls,
some praising, some condemning Singh;
some even asking for Kamala's hand in marriage.
Singh called himself the savior of the wolf girls,
and indeed it was by his efforts
Kamala lived to be about sixteen years old.
But he also made his own small reputation
by publishing a version of the wolf girls' tragic tale.

So what really happened?

No one knows for sure.

But now that you have read the story and looked at my notes and word lists, maybe you can solve the mystery of the wolf girls. Maybe one of the stories about how they were discovered seems right to you. Or maybe you'll come up with a theory of your own.

Just remember, as my dad always says: *Check Your Clues.*

1. Singh Told the Truth:

Wolves really did raise the girls. When Singh and his men found the children, killed the mother wolf, and brought Amala and Kamala to the orphanage, the girls displayed all the traits of wolf cubs.

How truthful or accurate do you think a journal written a year after the fact can be?

How are Indian wolf groups organized that might make them able to raise a human child?

What factors make it possible for Indian wolves to adopt two human children? Two human children of different ages?

How long would Kamala have had to live with wolves to lose all language?

Did the girls display any wolf traits?

2. Singh's Story Was a Complete Hoax:

The Reverend Singh was given two strange children by villagers, children who could neither speak nor walk. He decided to make up a story about rescuing them from wolves in order to make money for his orphanage.

Was Singh the kind of man to make up lies?

Were there good reasons for Singh to tell three different stories?

Were there scientists in India Singh could have called on?

What kind of cameras might have been available to a poor, disinherited missionary?

Why didn't Singh make careful scientific measurements?

What might Singh gain by such a hoax?

3. The Girls Were Simply Abandoned or Lost:

The girls had been abandoned or were lost in the sal forest. Before wolves could get to them, before they were bitten by snakes or savaged by tigers, before they starved, they were found and brought to The Home.

Can you find any scientific evidence to prove the existence of real feral children?

Is there evidence of children being abandoned in the forests of India?

Do wolves ever steal or kill humans, and if so, for what reason?

How long do you think a child might live safely in the sal forest?

4. The Girls Were Retarded, Handicapped, or Autistic:

Because the girls were autistic or retarded, they would always be a drain on a village economy or a wandering tribe's ability to move easily. They could never marry, bear children, or run a household. So their parents left them out in the field or delivered them to The Home.

Was abandoning children in fields or at the doorstep of an orphanage something that happened often in India?

Is their behavior explainable only as wolf behavior?

Is any of the girls' behavior similar to that of autistic or retarded children?

Were the wolf girls trainable?

Those are the four most popular explanations ever given. Are any of them right?

Nobody knows for sure. Not the police, not the lawyers, not the reporters, not the historians, and not even my dad. It is a mystery still waiting to be solved.

But I've got my own theory about what happened to the wolf girls of Midnapore, India.

And maybe—now—you do, too.